PEOPLE & PLACES

Mexico

972   Widdows,
W   Mexico.

29643   # 7060   15.00

Editor Steve Parker
Editor, U.S. Edition Joanne Fink
Designers Patrick Nugent, Bridget Morley
Photo-researcher Hugh Olliff
Studio services Kenneth Ward

A TEMPLAR BOOK

Devised and produced by Templar Publishing Ltd
107 High Street, Dorking, Surrey, England, RH4 1QA

Adapted and first published in the United States
in 1988 by Silver Burdett Press, Morristown, N.J.

Color separations by Positive Colour Ltd, Maldon, Essex, England
Printed by L.E.G.O., Vicenza, Italy

Library of Congress Cataloging-in-Publication Data

Widdows, Richard. 1947–
   Mexico / written by Richard Widdows : illustrated by Ann
Savage.
      p. cm. — (People and places)
   "A Templar book" — verso T.p.
   Includes index
   Summary: Text and pictures introduce the geography, history,
people, and culture of Mexico.
   ISBN 0-382-09506-5
1. Mexico—Juvenile literature.   [1. Mexico.]   I. Savage, Ann.
ill.   II. Title.   III. Series: People and places (Morristown, N.J.)
F1208.5W54 1988
972—dc19   87-28533
                                                  CIP
                                                  AC

Contents

WHERE IN THE WORLD ?

Which country is the 14th largest in the world? Which country is bigger than Britain, France, Spain, Italy, West Germany, and East Germany – all added together? Which country has the 13th largest population in the world? Which country is so hilly that half of its land is more than 3,200 feet above sea level? And which country has mountains always covered in snow, endless grassy prairies, dry-as-a-bone deserts, and thick, steamy tropical jungles?

The answer is *Los Estados Unidos Mexicanos* – the United Mexican States, or as we usually call it, Mexico. Its northern border with the United States is more than 2,000 miles long. Much of it is formed by the Rio Grande river. The southern border of 550 miles is with Guatemala and Belize.

People are often surprised to learn that Mexico is such a vast country, with every type of scenery, and that it has a long and colorful history, and rich culture.

Baja California
This peninsula, 750 miles long, is mostly remote deserts and rocky hills. From La Paz to Mexico City by road is almost 4,000 miles!

Symbols of Mexico

On Mexico's flag is an eagle on a cactus, holding a wriggling snake in its fearsome beak. In Aztec legend, the place where the eagle perched was the site where the Aztecs should build their city of Tenochtitlan (later to become Mexico City).

The ancient temples of the Toltecs and Aztecs were built in a flat-topped pyramid design with stepped sides.

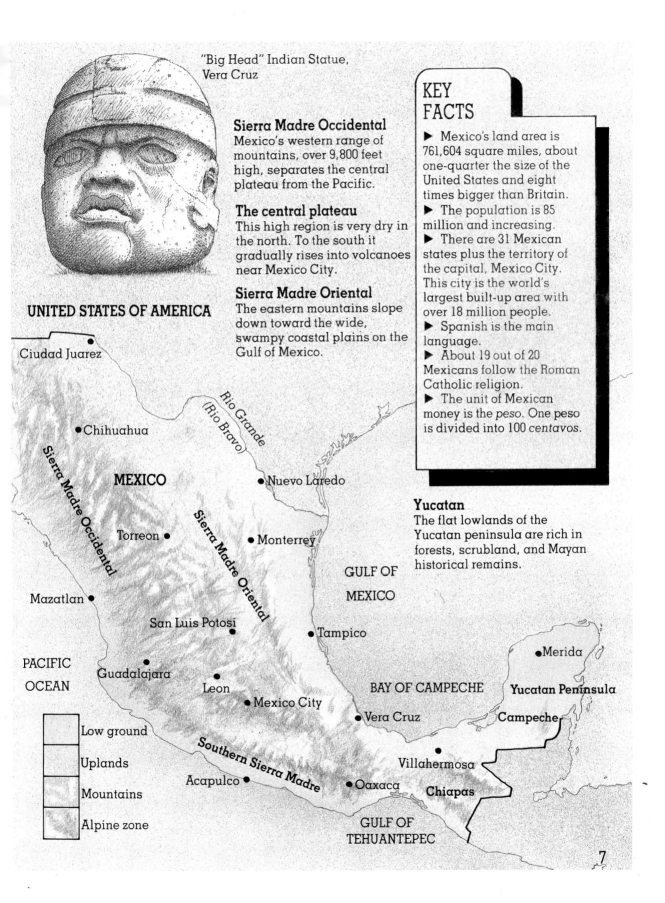

"Big Head" Indian Statue, Vera Cruz

Sierra Madre Occidental
Mexico's western range of mountains, over 9,800 feet high, separates the central plateau from the Pacific.

The central plateau
This high region is very dry in the north. To the south it gradually rises into volcanoes near Mexico City.

Sierra Madre Oriental
The eastern mountains slope down toward the wide, swampy coastal plains on the Gulf of Mexico.

KEY FACTS
▶ Mexico's land area is 761,604 square miles, about one-quarter the size of the United States and eight times bigger than Britain.
▶ The population is 85 million and increasing.
▶ There are 31 Mexican states plus the territory of the capital, Mexico City. This city is the world's largest built-up area with over 18 million people.
▶ Spanish is the main language.
▶ About 19 out of 20 Mexicans follow the Roman Catholic religion.
▶ The unit of Mexican money is the *peso*. One peso is divided into 100 *centavos*.

UNITED STATES OF AMERICA

Ciudad Juarez

Rio Grande (Rio Bravo)

Yucatan
The flat lowlands of the Yucatan peninsula are rich in forests, scrubland, and Mayan historical remains.

Chihuahua

MEXICO

Nuevo Laredo

Sierra Madre Occidental

Torreon

Sierra Madre Oriental

Monterrey

GULF OF MEXICO

Mazatlan

San Luis Potosi

Tampico

Merida

PACIFIC OCEAN

Guadalajara

Leon

Mexico City

BAY OF CAMPECHE

Yucatan Peninsula

Vera Cruz

Campeche

Low ground

Uplands

Mountains

Alpine zone

Southern Sierra Madre

Acapulco

Oaxaca

Villahermosa

Chiapas

GULF OF TEHUANTEPEC

A JOINING OF PEOPLES

Each year on October 12, Mexicans celebrate "The Day of the Race." It marks the beginning of the mixture of peoples, races, and cultures, that is now Mexico.

Many Indian tribes lived in Mexico before the Spaniards came in 1521. After the Spanish conquest many more Spaniards and other Europeans arrived in Mexico. They settled down to live, and formed mixed families with the Indians. Today, seven out of 10 modern Mexicans have mixed Indian and European ("Hispanic") ancestry and are called *mestizos*.

There are about four million true Mexican Indians. They belong to over 50 tribes and other groups, each with its own language and traditions. Most Indians live on the central plateau or the coastal plains. They are very loyal to their heritage, and Mexicans generally are much more proud of their Indian past than of their time under the Spanish conquerors.

Mexico's first lady

The Virgin of Guadalupe is the patron saint of Mexico. She symbolizes the joining of the Indian and Spanish ways of life. Her shrine in Mexico City is visited by six million pilgrims every year. Her picture appears on many of the banners carried at festivals and celebrations.

More people, bigger cities

Each year the population of Mexico rises by one and a half million. Over half the population is under 18 years of age. Three out of five Mexican people now live in towns, as families have had to leave the countryside and travel to the cities in search of work and money. Mexico City, shown here, is one of the world's fastest-growing cities.

Clothing

In cities and large towns Mexicans wear clothes similar to those worn by most Americans or Europeans. But, in the small villages, people wear the same kind of simple clothes that have been worn for hundreds of years. Men generally wear a shirt and trousers made of plain cotton, and leather sandals. A wide-brimmed hat called a *sombrero* gives protection from the hot sun. Women wear blouses, long skirts, and fringed shawls called *rebozos*. Leather chaps are worn when working on horseback.

HIGH PLAINS AND DUSTY DESERTS

In many "Western" movies, Mexico seems to be a hot, dry place. Spiky cactus plants dot the land while villagers struggle to grow crops in the thin, windblown soil. It is true that some northern parts of the country, such as the Sonora Desert, are like this. But Mexico's scenery is not just dust and cactus.

The amount of rain and the temperature vary widely across the country, mainly due to the difference in height of the land. Higher altitude means lower temperatures. On the central plateau, between 3,200 and 6,500 feet high, the climate is fresh and spring-like for most of the year.

The dry season is in winter and it always lives up to its name. But the "wet" season, in summer, often does not. Across the north of the country, and especially in the northwest, it remains very dry indeed. In some years only 2 inches of rain might fall. In the tropical southeast, a summer storm can bring 2 inches of rain in one day!

A spiky water bottle
The cactus is the typical desert plant of Mexico. It is well designed for living in hot, dry places as you can see from the picture opposite. Due to digging up by thoughtless plant collectors, some types of cacti are now very rare.

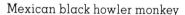
Mexican black howler monkey

Howlers and spiders
The Mexican black howler monkey can make one of the loudest noises of any animal. It lives in the forests and wooded grassland of Yucatan. The black-handed spider monkey dwells in the same region. It has enormously long arms and a prehensile tail. This kind of tail can be used to cling to the branches.

Spines keep away
plant-eating animals

Waxy skin cuts
down water loss

Swollen stem stores
water for long periods

Shallow roots quickly
absorb any rain that falls

North

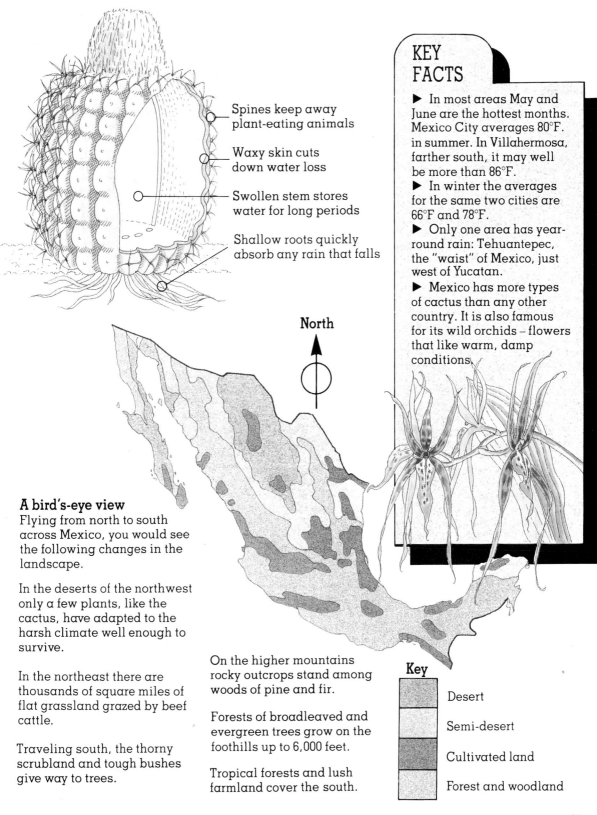

A bird's-eye view

Flying from north to south
across Mexico, you would see
the following changes in the
landscape.

In the deserts of the northwest
only a few plants, like the
cactus, have adapted to the
harsh climate well enough to
survive.

In the northeast there are
thousands of square miles of
flat grassland grazed by beef
cattle.

Traveling south, the thorny
scrubland and tough bushes
give way to trees.

On the higher mountains
rocky outcrops stand among
woods of pine and fir.

Forests of broadleaved and
evergreen trees grow on the
foothills up to 6,000 feet.

Tropical forests and lush
farmland cover the south.

Key

Desert

Semi-desert

Cultivated land

Forest and woodland

11

A PARADISE FOR WILDLIFE

Mexico can be a nature-lover's paradise. It has almost every type of country, from rocky deserts in the north to thick, steamy jungles in the south. Wild plants and animals thrive in the mountains and remote areas which are not suitable for farmland.

Unlike some other countries, such as Kenya, Mexico does not rely on its wildlife to attract tourists. However, "nature vacations" are on the increase, especially in the Baja California and Yucatan regions. People come to watch the flocks of pink flamingoes on the northern shores of the Yucatan, the multicolored parrots and macaws in the forests, and the agile monkeys of the Chiapas woodlands.

The crystal clear water of Cozumel, an island off the Yucatan coast, is one of the best places in the world to scuba dive. People now swim among the colorful coral and enjoy watching the exotic fish, rather than catching and killing them.

KEY FACTS

Mexico is home to an amazing variety of creatures. There are:
► more than 500 different kinds, or species, of mammal,
► over 1,400 species of bird,
► at least 680 different reptile species,
► and more than 260 species of amphibian,
► as well as orchids and cacti of almost every variety.

The migrating monarch
Monarch butterflies make a twice-yearly trip from the northern United States and Canada, down to the southern states and Mexico. Recently, it was found that millions of monarchs spend the winter in a forest in central Mexico.

Poisonous lizards

There are only two kinds of poisonous lizards in the world, and they both live in Mexico. The Mexican beaded lizard is so named because its rounded scales look like Indian strung beads. It comes from western Mexico and grows to nearly three feet long.

The Gila monster is the other poisonous lizard. It is a close relation of the beaded lizard, and has the same rounded scales. Its bite is very painful but is unlikely to kill a healthy person. The Gila also lives in dry, rocky areas of western Mexico.

Gray whale and calf

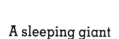

Gila monster

A big baby

One of Mexico's most famous animals is the gray whale. Each winter hundreds of baby gray whales are born in the warm waters off Baja California. Each baby weighs over half a ton and drinks over 50 gallons of its mother's milk each day. In spring the whales migrate north to their feeding grounds in the Arctic Ocean. Fifty years ago gray whales were in danger of becoming extinct, but mass hunting is now banned and these mammals are safe.

A sleeping giant

Popocatepetl, 17,887 feet high, is a dormant ("sleeping") volcano, about 43 miles southeast of Mexico City. Its peak is always snow-capped, and its lower slopes are a haven for wildlife.

THE VACATION OF A LIFETIME

Tourism is second only to oil for bringing foreign money into Mexico. The country has spectacular scenery, beautiful beaches, fine food, and friendly people. For tourists from all over the world, especially Europe and Asia, Mexico offers the vacation of a lifetime.

Nearly nine out of 10 visitors to Mexico come from the U.S. and Canada. They visit mostly the northern parts of the country, just over the border. In one year recently, about seven million American tourists made short trips from California, Arizona, New Mexico, and Texas. They spent more money in Mexico than everyone else in the whole country put together.

Since the mid-1970s the Mexican government has encouraged tourism through its own agency, FONTAUR. They are eager to tell people about their country's ancient cultures and historic towns, as well as the already-famous seaside resorts and the attractions of Mexico City.

Fun time in Tijuana

The boom town of Tijuana (say it "tee-wanna"), in Mexico's northwestern corner, is home for more than a million people. It is only half an hour's drive from San Diego in southern California. Americans who cross the border enter a world of unusual colors and tastes, and every kind of entertainment from gambling to bullfighting.

Acapulco – the place to go

Acapulco is known all over the world as an exotic and exciting place to go on vacation. The all-year sunshine and sweeping sandy bay attract more than three million visitors each year.

Acapulco is an Indian word meaning "the place where the reeds were destroyed." Tourism often has bad effects, such as ruining areas for wildlife and filling the landscape with ugly hotels. But the tourist industry brings much-needed work and money for the Mexican people, from restaurant owners to local farmers, guides and taxi drivers, from hotel managers to cooks and cleaners.

Traditional dancing

Mexico is famous for its festivals and colorful carnivals. These Indian dancers in traditional feathered costumes are celebrating the festival of the Virgin of Guadalupe, in Mexico City.

Going for a dip?

The cliffs of La Quebrada, at Acapulco, are used as a diving board by skilled youngsters. It is more than 130 feet from the cliff top to the shallow water, as high as a 15-story building. The cliffs jut out slightly so that the divers must jump outward several yards. At night this dangerous scene is lit by torches and watched by guests in nearby hotels.

USING THE LAND AND THE SEA

Most places in Mexico are too mountainous or too dry for farming. Only about one-tenth of the land area is suitable for growing crops. So Mexico has to buy huge amounts of basic foods from abroad, mainly from the United States.

In the countryside, many farms are small and run by one family. The people grow a few crops and keep a few goats, chickens, pigs, and sheep. Water for irrigation is scarce, and piping it to the farmers' fields would cost too much money. Fertilizers, tractors, and combine harvesters are also too costly for most farmers. In the northwest, near the United States, there are some large, modern farms. These grow fruits and vegetables for sale across the border.

Almost one-third of Mexico is covered by woodlands, but it is only recently that the trees have been used for timber. The most valuable trees are the pines and other conifers that grow in the center of the country. These are cut and made into pulp for paper, or are used in buildings and furniture.

Sugar cane

Mexico's main crops
The amounts of crops have increased tremendously in the past 20 years. Besides those shown here, Mexican farmers grow alfalfa, tobacco, tomatoes, melons, and a valuable new crop – coffee. Cotton used to be important but it is now grown less and less.

CROP	AMOUNT PRODUCED EACH YEAR
Corn	16.7 million tons
Sorghum	7 million tons
Wheat	3.5 million tons
Beans	1.6 million tons
Soya	.8 million tons
Rice	.7 million tons

16

Sapodilla fruit

A fact to chew over...
Sapodilla trees grow in the Yucatan area. They are "tapped" by cutting a V-shaped slit in the bark. Out of this oozes a sticky gum called *chicle*, which is sent to factories in the United States to be made into chewing gum.

Sliced sugar cane

Life on the plantation
Mexico is the world's fourth-largest producer of sugar cane. Harvesting the cane is backbreaking work and often pays poorly.

Anchovies

Tough and stringy
Sisal is a tall plant with strong fibers in its stem. The fibers are woven into sackcloth, ropes, brushes, and rough rugs. Over half of the world's sisal crop comes from Mexico's Yucatan area.

Foods from the sea
In the 1970s the Mexican government began a huge program to catch more fish from the rich seas around Mexico. The program was very successful and Mexico is now one of the top 10 fishing nations. Much sea food is exported. Jumbo shrimp are fished from the waters off Oaxaca and are hardly seen by Mexicans. They are exported to the United States and Europe.

17

TRADING IN THE WORLD MARKET

Mexico is a big country. It handles similar amounts of trade to Australia or Spain. Around nine-tenths of imports to Mexico are foods and raw materials for industry. Mexican goods and services form one-quarter of all those produced by Central and South America.

Mexico buys over three-fifths of its imports from the United States. It sells back to the Americans over three-fifths of its exports. Business in Mexico relies heavily on its giant northern neighbor. The U.S. economy is over 20 times larger than Mexico's.

Mexico is in debt. It owes billions of dollars to world banks, to repay the money it borrowed to build houses, factories, and roads. However, massive amounts of oil were discovered in the country recently and the tourist trade is increasing rapidly. Hopefully now Mexico's economy is on the road to recovery.

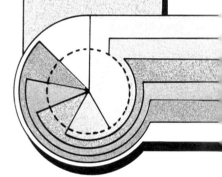

Imports

Main regions selling to Mexico:
U.S.A.
Europe
    (mainly Spain)
Japan
Central and
    South America

Mining metals

Mexico mines and refines more silver than any other country. It also produces much zinc and lead (sixth largest producer for each) as well as copper, steel and sulphur. Here silver goods are on sale in the town of Taxco, between Mexico City and Acapulco, which was the "Silver City" of the Spanish colonial days.

Mexico's ins and outs

The main imports to Mexico, and the country's chief exports, are shown in the diagram below. The colored portions in the circles represent the relative values of each import and export. Crude oil is by far the largest export, providing about half of all the income from goods sold abroad.

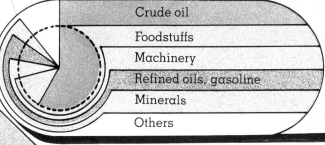

Exports

Main regions buying from Mexico:

U.S.A.
Central and
 South America
Europe
 (mainly Spain)
Japan

Crude oil
Foodstuffs
Machinery
Refined oils, gasoline
Minerals
Others

Machinery
Foodstuffs
Chemicals
Iron and steel products
Car parts
Others

Going back underground

The mines of La Valencia, near Leon, yielded much silver when the Spanish ruled Mexico. Then the mines were closed. Recently, new techniques and discoveries have meant that, once again, it is worth mining the silver. La Valencia has reopened and new buildings have been constructed.

OIL AND INDUSTRY

Oil was discovered in Mexico at the beginning of this century. At first, only small amounts were used as a raw material in industry and as a source of heat and electricity. Gradually, however, oil became more important in industry. In 1972 more oil was found, then more, and more ... By 1984 Mexico had become the fourth-largest oil producer, in a world thirsty for oil in any and every industrial process.

Massive new reserves of oil are still being discovered in Mexico, enough to last 100 years even at the present rate. There are also huge reserves of natural gas. So Mexico has no need to buy oil from other countries.

If Mexico is rich in oil, why isn't it a rich country? In order to pay for the exploration, drilling, oil rigs, pipelines, and refineries, the Mexicans borrowed gigantic sums of money. They intended to pay back the loans when the oil started to flow in quantity. But during the 1970s, people throughout the world used less oil. This made oil prices go down. Mexico was unable to sell its oil for the money it had hoped, so it couldn't pay back the loans.

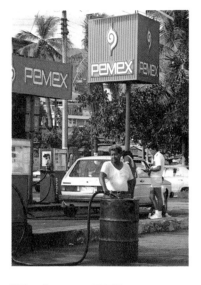

PEtroleum in MEXico
In Mexico the exploration, drilling, and refining of oil is carried out by the state-run PEMEX corporation. PEMEX employs more people and invests more money than any other company in the country.

The refining business
In the past most of Mexico's crude oil (oil straight from the well) was shipped abroad in tankers. Refineries in other countries purified the crude oil into gasoline and industrial chemicals. However, the Mexicans have recently built their own oil refineries, like the one on the skyline here. Mexico now refines almost one-half of its crude oil, and this proportion is rising all the time.

KEY FACTS

Industry needs energy, and Mexico has abundant supplies of this.

▶ The nation's own oil and natural gas provide nine-tenths of its energy needs.

▶ Along the steep eastern and southern edges of the central plateau, dams across rivers produce hydro-electricity.

▶ Also on the central plateau, the hot springs can be used to create "geothermal" power.

▶ The demand for electricity in Mexico more than doubled between 1970 and 1980.

▶ Most energy is produced and used in the center of the country, around Mexico City. Many country areas have no electricity or gas supplies.

A sea of oil

Two-thirds of Mexico's oil comes from under the sea, in the Bay of Campeche. It is thought that as much again could lie under the ground, in the Chiapas region to the south.

OUT AND ABOUT IN MEXICO

Traveling around Mexico has always been difficult. There are few rivers suitable for ships, and the mountains make it difficult to build good roads and railways. Over the past 30 years, however, great improvements have been made. More than two million people now have jobs in the road and rail industries.

Mexico has more than 160,000 miles of surfaced roads and at least the same length of unsurfaced dirt or dust tracks. The roads carry four-fifths of all freight in the country, while 97 passengers out of 100 travel by bus or car. Railways are a poor second.

In such a big country, flying is the fastest way to get around. Mexico has about 30 international airports, another 20 major airports, and nearly 1,400 small airstrips! Two-fifths of all air passengers fly with Mexican-owned airlines.

Slow but cheap
The railways have suffered from lack of funds and passengers. About 50 years ago there were over 8,700 miles of track. Today there are less than 8,100 miles. Rail travel is slower and less reliable than bus – though it is cheaper.

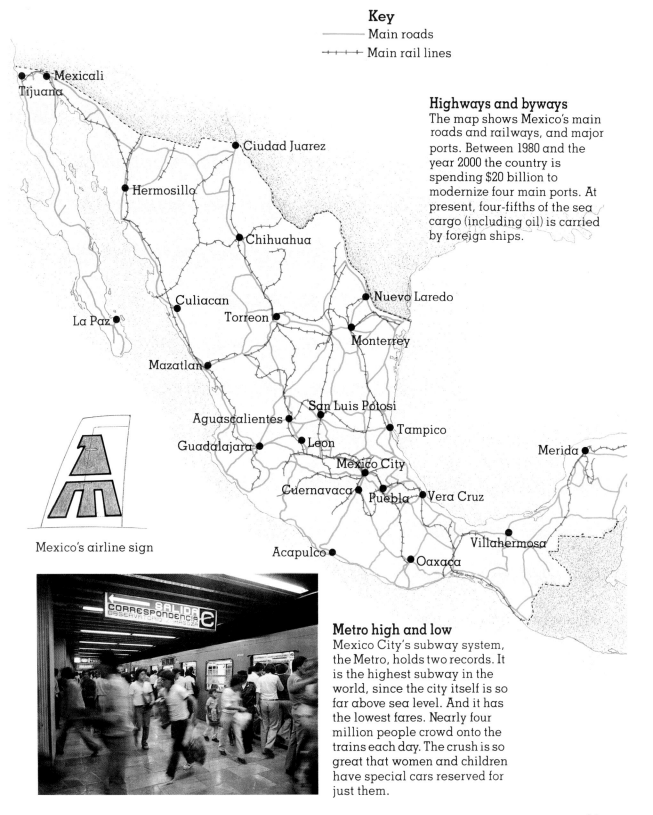

Highways and byways

The map shows Mexico's main roads and railways, and major ports. Between 1980 and the year 2000 the country is spending $20 billion to modernize four main ports. At present, four-fifths of the sea cargo (including oil) is carried by foreign ships.

Mexicali
Tijuana
Ciudad Juarez
Hermosillo
Chihuahua
Culiacan
Torreon
Nuevo Laredo
Monterrey
La Paz
Mazatlan
Aguascalientes
San Luis Potosi
Tampico
Guadalajara
Leon
Merida
Mexico City
Cuernavaca
Puebla
Vera Cruz
Villahermosa
Acapulco
Oaxaca

Mexico's airline sign

Metro high and low

Mexico City's subway system, the Metro, holds two records. It is the highest subway in the world, since the city itself is so far above sea level. And it has the lowest fares. Nearly four million people crowd onto the trains each day. The crush is so great that women and children have special cars reserved for just them.

THE GIANT GROWS

Mexico is the largest city in the world. It is home to almost 20 million people – and it is still growing at an alarming rate.

Mexico City is a mixture of past, present, and future. It is built on the site of Tenochtitlan, the Aztecs' ancient capital. Today it is the center of Mexican government, industry, culture, and leisure. It is also the key to the nation's future. Over half the inhabitants are under 18 years old, and every week around 10,000 more people arrive in search of work.

The city is filled with contrasts. Wealthy business tycoons live in fabulous mansions, while a few miles away the wooden shacks, home for the city's poorer people, stretch as far as you can see. They have no water supplies or electricity or sewage. In the center of the city fashionable stores sell the best in jewels and perfumes, while the city dumps swarm with children searching for bits of food and clothing. Yet the people are very proud of their capital.

KEY FACTS

▶ It is estimated that 30 million people will be living in Mexico City by the year 2000.

▶ The built-up area covers roughly 775 square miles – about one-thousandth of the area of the country. Yet one-fifth of all Mexicans live there.

▶ One family in three sleeps together in a single room. Most families have from three to five children.

▶ Over 30,000 factories in and near the city account for over half of Mexico's industry.

▶ Unlike many other great cities, Mexico City has no main river. Water is pumped up from the former lake bed and other pumps work day and night to bring in more drinking water.

▶ Because of the soft soil and pumping, parts of the city sink almost a foot each year.

Spread of the shanties
Millions of people in Mexico City live in shacks made of bits of wood, metal sheeting or even cardboard. Many children have no proper schooling and families survive from day to day as best they can.

Three cultures

The Plaza of the Three Cultures in the northern part of the city shows three phases of the nation's history. The ruined pyramid is where Hernan Cortes, the Spanish invader, finally beat the Aztecs. Santiago Church and the Convent of the Cross date from the Spanish period. The tall modern building is the Secretariat of Foreign Relations.

Key

1 El Angel (Independence Monument)
2 Monument to the Revolution
3 Cathedral
4 National Palace
5 Chapultepec Castle

A mosaic on the wall of Mexico City's University Library

MEXICO IN ANCIENT TIMES

People have lived in Mexico for many centuries. Prehistoric remains show that the first settlers arrived around 20,000 years ago, as part of the great human migration southward through North and South America.

Farming probably began in Mexico about 8,000 years ago. Fruits and crops such as avocados were followed by corn and beans. These early farmers used stone axes and wooden digging sticks to work the land. Cotton was being woven into cloth about 5,000 years ago, and potters were at work 4,000 years ago.

Mexico saw many different groups and cultures, from the time of the Olmecs, around 3,200 years ago, until the Spaniards arrived in 1519. Sadly, much of Mexico's rich tribal culture was destroyed by the invaders. Many aspects of the country's past are now lost for ever.

Key to ancient cities

- Olmec
- Mayan
- Teotihuacanos
- Zapotec/Mixtec
- Toltec
- ▲ Aztec
- Aztec Empire

An example of Mixtec picture writing

The Zapotecs and Mixtecs

Based in the Valley of Oaxaca, the Zapotecs were talented craftsmen. For 500 years their great city of Monte Alban dominated the area. It had rich palaces, temples, tombs, and houses for more than 30,000 people. By 1,200 years ago Monte Alban had fallen into ruin as the Mixtecs took over. Like the Zapotecs, the Mixtecs lived in the Valley of Oaxaca. They made fabulous jewelry of gold, silver, and jade which they buried in the tombs of their noblemen. They took over the Zapotec lands. Then, about 500 years ago, they themselves were conquered by the Aztecs.

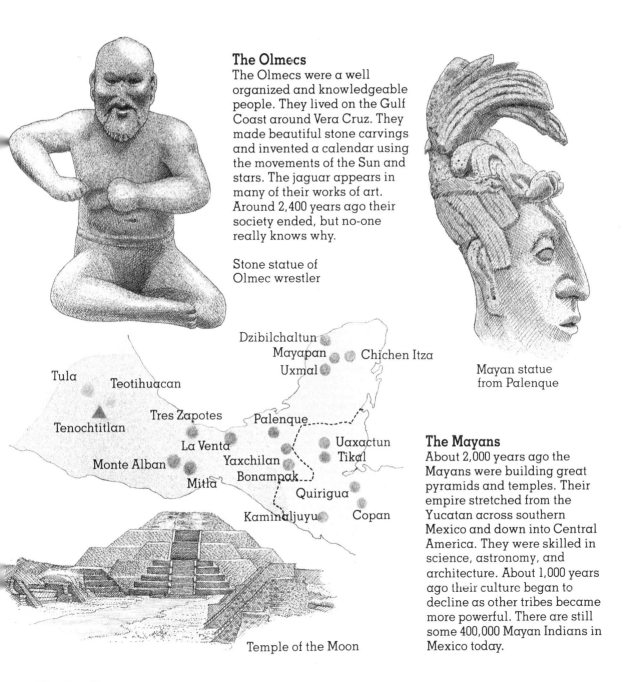

The Olmecs
The Olmecs were a well organized and knowledgeable people. They lived on the Gulf Coast around Vera Cruz. They made beautiful stone carvings and invented a calendar using the movements of the Sun and stars. The jaguar appears in many of their works of art. Around 2,400 years ago their society ended, but no-one really knows why.

Stone statue of
Olmec wrestler

Mayan statue
from Palenque

Dzibilchaltun
Mayapan
Chichen Itza
Uxmal

Tula
Teotihuacan

Tres Zapotes
Palenque

Tenochtitlan

La Venta
Uaxactun
Tikal

Monte Alban
Yaxchilan
Bonampak

Mitla

Quirigua

Kaminaljuyu
Copan

Temple of the Moon

The Mayans
About 2,000 years ago the Mayans were building great pyramids and temples. Their empire stretched from the Yucatan across southern Mexico and down into Central America. They were skilled in science, astronomy, and architecture. About 1,000 years ago their culture began to decline as other tribes became more powerful. There are still some 400,000 Mayan Indians in Mexico today.

The Teotihuacanos
This tribe built the legendary Temples of the Sun and Moon in the Valley of Mexico, near where Mexico City is today. Their city of 200,000 people lasted from about 2,300 to 1,300 years ago. But exactly who they were, and what happened to them, is still a mystery.

The Toltecs
These fierce people conquered much of Mexico from their base at Tula. They collected "taxes" in the form of food from the tribes they ruled. They were powerful about 1,000 years ago, but by 800 years ago their society was crumbling.

WORSHIPERS OF THE SUN

The Aztecs were the last in a long line of Indian groups who conquered and ruled over most of Mexico. They tend to be the best known because they held power at the time of the Spanish invasion.

The Aztecs were originally a nomadic tribe from the north of Mexico but, in 1345, after two centuries of wandering, they eventually settled in the Valley of Mexico. They were a fierce and warlike people and they soon defeated the other tribes living there. By 1430 they had built two huge cities on islands in the shallow Lake Texcoco. One was Tlatelolco, a busy center for trade.

Causeways ran over the lake to the other city, Tenochtitlan, the Aztec capital. This had fine palaces and temples. More than 300,000 people lived in and around the cities.

When Cortes and his Spanish followers arrived in 1519, they were amazed at the size of the Aztec empire. The ruler, Montezuma II, controlled more people than many European kings and emperors.

Aztec gods

The Aztecs worshiped several gods. The main one was Huitzilopochtli, god of sun and war. Tlaloc was the rain god, and the snake-like Quetzalcoatl was god of art and beauty and of the mind. The Aztecs believed that the gods always threatened to destroy them. Only by sacrificing animals and people, sometimes by tearing out their hearts, would the gods be kept satisfied. The priests thought that if the sun god did not receive regular sacrifices, he might not rise the next day.

Huitzilopochtli   Tlaloc   Quetzalcoatl

Lake gardens
Food for people in the cities was grown on *chinampas*, plots covered with rich mud from the bed of Lake Texcoco. Thousands of these "island gardens" dotted the waters of the lake. Today the gardens are a popular attraction for visitors.

Absolute ruler
Emperor Montezuma's word was law. It is said that every day he could choose from 1,000 meals which had been cooked specially for him. He was more interested in religious duties then warfare. This Spanish painting from 1600 shows Montezuma meeting the Spanish explorer Cortes.

THE REIGN OF SPAIN

The defeat of the mighty Aztecs by the Spanish explorer Hernan Cortes and his 700 soldiers is one of the strangest tales in history. In 1519 Cortes and his 11 ships arrived in Mexico from Cuba. Two years later Montezuma lay dead, the Aztec capital lay in ruins, and the Spaniards controlled the nation.

During and after the conquest one-third of the Indians in Mexico were killed, starved to death, or died from diseases brought by the Europeans. The Spaniards burned thousands of books and destroyed many treasures from 3,000 years of Mexican culture. It was a terrible loss to the country.

The Spaniards set up their own government and took much of the precious gems and metals out of the country. They introduced Christianity, and for three centuries they ruled their colony of "New Spain."

Eventually, the Mexicans revolted. Encouraged by the success of the American Revolution and the French Revolution, they turned on their European masters. The bloody Mexican revolution lasted 11 years and cost over half a million lives, but the Mexican people won. In 1821 Mexico was declared independent and the Federal Republic of Mexico finally came into being two years later.

Why did the Aztecs lose?

There are many reasons why Cortes and his followers defeated the Aztec army, even though it was many times stronger.

▶ When the Spaniards landed at Vera Cruz, Cortes ordered their ships to be destroyed. The Spanish knew there was no going back.

▶ Many tribes in Mexico hated being ruled by the fierce Aztecs. They were only too ready to help the newcomers.

▶ The Aztecs were terrified of guns and horses, which they had never seen before.

▶ The invaders strongly believed that what they were doing was for the good of their religion, Christianity. They were also very greedy for the fabulous Aztec treasures.

▶ At first Montezuma was friendly toward the Spaniards. During this time many Indians caught diseases carried by the invaders, such as smallpox, and died.

▶ Cortes was a cunning and inspiring leader. Montezuma, on the other hand, was not. At first he believed the ancient prophecy had come true: Cortes was the god Quetzalcoatl, come to take away his throne.

Cortes and his soldiers ride behind Christ's cross

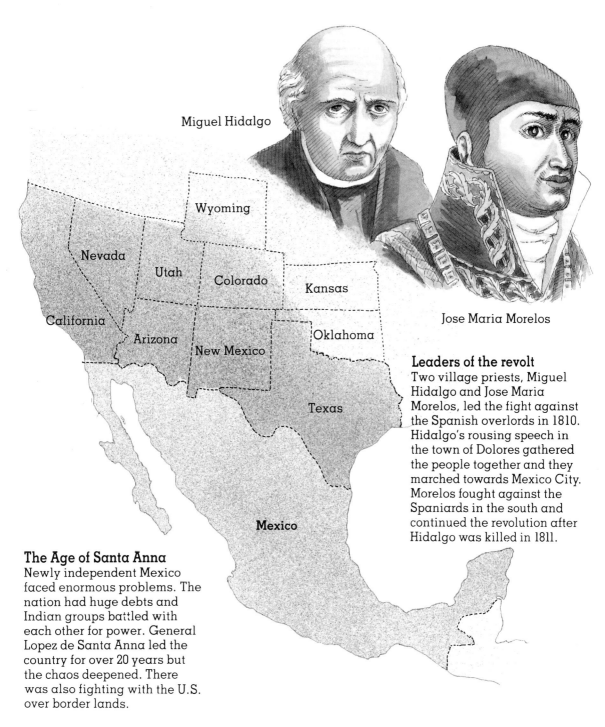

Miguel Hidalgo

Jose Maria Morelos

Wyoming

Nevada

Utah

Colorado

Kansas

California

Arizona

New Mexico

Oklahoma

Texas

Mexico

Leaders of the revolt

Two village priests, Miguel Hidalgo and Jose Maria Morelos, led the fight against the Spanish overlords in 1810. Hidalgo's rousing speech in the town of Dolores gathered the people together and they marched towards Mexico City. Morelos fought against the Spaniards in the south and continued the revolution after Hidalgo was killed in 1811.

The Age of Santa Anna

Newly independent Mexico faced enormous problems. The nation had huge debts and Indian groups battled with each other for power. General Lopez de Santa Anna led the country for over 20 years but the chaos deepened. There was also fighting with the U.S. over border lands.

Mexican land

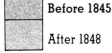

Before 1845

After 1848

Disappearing Mexico

Mexico and the U.S. quarreled continually about the land on the border between them, particularly Texas. After several battles the Americans forced the Mexicans to give in and sell them more than half their country – lands that are now Texas, California, New Mexico, and other southwestern states.

THE BIRTH OF THE NEW MEXICO

Exactly 100 years after the Mexican revolution, against the Spanish, there was a second one. This time it was against General Porfirio Diaz and his government, which had come to power in 1876. Some progress had been made in the country, with new mines and factories opening and railways and roads being built. The nation had become richer, but the people could see that the new wealth was not being shared. They wanted to elect a new government, and in 1910 their fight began.

The second Mexican revolution was a long and bitter struggle. Many times the fighting seemed to be over, only to start again. Thousands of Mexicans died and others fled north over the border.

Mexico could not be changed overnight. The promises made by the leaders of the revolution were gradually put into action when Lazaro Cardenas became President in 1934. After World War II, President Miguel Aleman Valdes continued the reforms from 1946 to 1952. By the 1960s Mexico's economic miracle was happening at last.

Did the revolution work?
In Mexico today, peasant farmers still work the land to scrape a living for their families. Although famine and starvation are rare, luxuries are few in many country regions.

Pancho Villa

Emiliano Zapata

Heroes of the revolution

Many groups fought in the Mexican revolution. In the south, people flocked to join Emiliano Zapata, a Zapotec Indian farmer from Moreles. He was a good leader and his army of peasant farmers were willing to die for their cause. Zapata was murdered in 1919.

In the north, the people's hero was Francisco "Pancho" Villa, a bandit from Durango. His army of cowboys attacked the homes of many wealthy families. In 1914 Zapata and Villa marched into Mexico City at the head of 50,000 peasant soldiers – but still the fighting continued.

FUN AND GAMES IN MEXICO

Soccer is the most popular sport in Mexico, both for players and spectators. Next comes bullfighting and the Mexican-style rodeos, *charreadas*, which have developed from sports brought to Mexico by the Spanish conquerors.

There are over 220 permanent bullrings in the country, and probably twice as many makeshift ones. From September to December is the "little season" for less experienced *matadors* (bullfighters). The experts perform in the "big season" from November to April.

Fishing is an enormously popular pastime. If you have the money you can hire a boat and go deep-sea fishing for shark and marlin. Many Mexicans, as well as tourists, enjoy swimming, surfing, and windsurfing.

It's *charreadas* time!

The Mexican rodeo is a colorful and exciting event, usually held on Sunday mornings. Most towns have a rodeo ring. The *charros* show their skills, performing amazing tricks on horseback and roping the bull with the *reata* (Mexican lasso). The competitions and displays are combined with feasting, singing, and dancing.

The fastest ball game

Like bullfighting, the ball game *jai-alai* or "pelota" came from Spain. It is played with a hard rubber ball and a sling-shaped wicker bat tied to the wrist, on a three-sided court over 160 feet long. It is said to be the fastest ball game in the world – the ball travels at about 160 miles per hour. The main courts are in Mexico City and Tijuana.

Sunday afternoon sport

Bullfighting seems cruel and dangerous to some people, but to most Mexicans it is a way of life. It has been banned twice in the past, but each time it returned more popular than ever. An average of one in four matadors will be crippled in the ring, while one in 10 will be killed. Mexico City's *Plaza de Mexico* bullring is the largest in the world, holding 50,000 people.

EATING AND DRINKING

Many of the things we eat and drink first came from Mexico. Turkeys, corn (maize), beans and avocados, tomatoes and chili peppers, peanuts, and vanilla flavoring all came originally from Mexico. *Cacao*, the seed from which cocoa and chocolate is made, was being harvested by Mexican Indians hundreds of years ago.

Mexican food has a reputation for being hot and spicy. Most meals are flavored with chilis, peppers and other spices and herbs, and served with a rich sauce.

Many Mexican states have their own special dishes. Oaxaca and Puebla are famous for their *moles*, sauces made from 30 or more ingredients including chili and chocolate! Chicken, turkey, and other meats are cooked slowly in the *mole*, often with nuts for extra flavor.

Coffee is a popular drink, traditionally as *café de olla* brewed with cinnamon and sugar and served in small earthenware cups. *Chocolate caliente* (hot chocolate drink) is also a great favorite.

Time for a tequila!
Tequila is a town of about 30,000 people, some 30 miles west of the city of Guadalajara. *Tequila* is also the name of Mexico's famous strong alcoholic drink. It's made from the distilled and fermented juice of the blue maguey shown here, a type of agave (a cactus-like plant). The town of Tequila has more than 20 distilleries that make the tequila drink, and there are many other distilleries making similar drinks across the nation. Cactus juice is also fermented to make beer-like *pulque*.

Eating the Mexican way

Most Mexicans are not rich and their style of cooking makes a little meat go a long way. The food is often very healthy, with beans providing fiber, and fruits and vegetables providing vitamins. Meals are eaten at almost any time of day. Mexican families often get together in each other's homes for food and drink, talk and laughter.

Some favorite foods

Tortilla A soft, warm pancake made from corn or wheat flour. Eaten at almost every meal.
Taco Tortilla folded or rolled up with a spicy filling inside.
Frijoles Beans, usually red or black kidney beans or rosecoco beans.
Chilis Chili peppers of various sorts which give a spicy-hot "sting" to many Mexican dishes.
Enchilada Tortilla rolled or folded and filled with cheese, tomatoes and so on (not usually meat) and dipped in or covered with sauce.

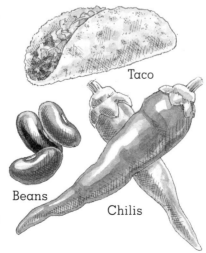

Taco

Beans

Chilis

Tamale Light, fluffy corn dumpling steamed in a corn husk and filled with meat, fish, turkey, and just about everything.
Chile con Carne Meat, beans, tomatoes, onions, chilis, spices, and various other ingredients simmered together. Although famous it's not truly Mexican, but an American version of Mexican food.

THE INDIAN WAY OF LIFE

Before the Spanish conquest more than 20 million Indians, from dozens of different tribes, lived in what is now Mexico. Those who survived the conquest – and the diseases brought by the Europeans – lived mainly in the dry north or the mountainous south. Today there are about four million true Indians, living mostly in the same remote areas.

Today, the Mayans, with about 400,000 members, are one of the largest Indian groups. In their home of the Chiapas highlands they keep up many of their traditions in clothes, festivals, dancing, and religion.

Mexico is proud of its Indian past (see page 8). However, many Mexican Indians today have a difficult life. They rarely own the land they farm. Few of them get a good education or a well-paid job. It is often difficult for them to combine the ancient Indian ways with, for example, modern farming methods and medicine.

The Huichols

Experts say that these Indians, more than any other original peoples, have preserved their way of life and are the least changed by the modern world. They live in the mountains of northern Jalisco, near the Pacific coast. They worship fire and the deer, and during ceremonies they wear magnificent headdresses made of feathers.

The Totonacs

The Totonacs are about 150,000 in number. They come from around Vera Cruz and Puebla. In their ceremony "The Dance of the Fly," four men hang upside down from a giant pole and make interweaving patterns as they swing around and down the pole to the ground. They symbolize the four elements of fire, earth, water, and air.

Signalling the homecoming
A Huichol Indian blows on his horn during a celebration. He is signaling the return of his tribe's pilgrims from a religious festival.

The Tarahumaras
In the Sonora desert of the north and the mountains of Chihuahua, live several tribes, including the Tarahumaras. They grow corn, live in caves or build houses (like the one shown here) from sun-dried clay bricks, and weave clothes and rugs much as their ancestors did. In some areas they make a living by selling their crafts to tourists.

ALL IN THE FAMILY

In Mexico people live in all sorts of ways – from ancient Indian lifestyles to modern Western ones. For many Mexicans, though, life is traditionally centered around the family home. And in Mexico the family includes grandparents, aunts and uncles, cousins and godparents, as well as parents and children. Family ties are very strong.

In traditional Mexican home life the father is the head of the family. He earns the money and he makes important decisions concerning his children's schooling and behavior. The mother cooks, cleans, and takes care of her family's health and welfare.

Mexican children are taught to be polite and respectful to their elders. They should help and work together for the good of the family. Of course some children are naughty, just like anywhere else!

Times are changing in Mexico, as they are in other countries. More and more young women are making their own careers, and fewer are marrying young and raising a family. For the modern city-dweller with a good job, life can be similar to that in any big city around the world.

What's in a name?

In keeping with Spanish tradition, a Mexican usually has a first name and then two family names. The father's family name is first and is the one most often used. The second name is the mother's family name.

Out on the town

The square or *plaza* of a typical country town is the center of business and social life. Important buildings, shops, and cafes are grouped around it, and people meet there to talk and have refreshments. On Sunday evening in some towns it is traditional for older boys to walk one way around the square while girls walk the other way, under the watchful eyes of their parents.

Center of the home

The *patio* is the focus of family life. A typical Mexican house is built around a central patio, open to the sky, and surrounded by the kitchen, living rooms, and bedrooms. Some older buildings have a shared central courtyard, as shown here.

'Til death us do part

A Mexican girl looks forward to two important days. One is her 15th birthday, when she leaves childhood behind and becomes a *señorita*, a young woman. The other great day is her wedding day, a cause for celebration, feasting, and dancing.

41

PAINTINGS ON THE WALLS

The ancient peoples of Mexico had a strong tradition of artistry and craftsmanship. They made statues, carvings, paintings, and jewelry of great beauty. The mysterious Olmecs carved giant heads, weighing up to 45 tons, with faces oddly more Black-like than Mexican.

The Mayans produced complex writing using a mixture of pictures, dots, and squiggles. They wrote thousands of books using paper made from vegetable fibers. All but four of these were destroyed during the Spanish invasion. The buildings at Tula, the Toltec capital, are decorated with images of warriors, jaguars, eagles, and the plumed serpent god, Quetzalcoatl.

The ancient buildings of the Indians and the churches of the Spanish period often had large scenes painted on their walls, called murals. The giant murals of modern buildings in Mexico show scenes from the Indian and Spanish past. Murals are now seen as a very "Mexican" form of art.

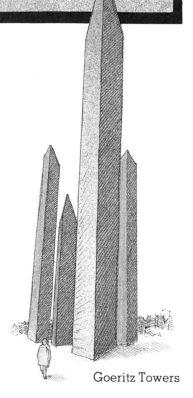

Goeritz Towers

Steel, glass, and concrete

Modern skyscrapers and office buildings in Mexican cities look much the same as in any other country. But there are some very unusual designs. In Campeche there are two futuristic buildings known locally as "the jukebox" and "the flying saucer." The Goeritz Towers are at the entrance to Mexico City's Satellite Town.

Land of murals

Diego Rivera was a Mexican painter. In the 1920s and 30s he helped to make murals popular again across the world. Rivera worked in other countries, especially the United States. In this mural, painted in 1942, Rivera shows the ancient Tarascan Indians.

► It is said that there are 365 main fiestas in Mexico. That's one for each day of the year!

► December 12 is a national holiday to honor the Virgin of Guadalupe (see page 8).

► Christmas is a mixture of old and new customs. Some children write to Father Christmas and receive presents. There are processions to commemorate Mary and Joseph's search for the inn at Bethlehem.

► In the early hours of November 1 many Mexicans believe that the souls of dead children visit the family home. It is called "The Day of the Dead." Presents, cakes, and sweets are left out for them.

Music and fiesta

Almost every day there is a big festival somewhere in Mexico. The people dress up and there is music and dance, feasting, parades, and carnival floats, processions, contests, and street entertainment. In smaller towns the festival day is as important as Christmas or Easter.

The craft market

The crafts for sale at local markets are mainly for tourists. The handicrafts, jewelry, blankets, and wooden carvings are carefully made to traditional Indian designs.

43

TOMORROW'S MEXICO

Mexico certainly faces its fair share of problems. The nation owes great sums of money to other countries, and its oil and gas are worth less in today's world. Its population is growing at an alarming rate, and daily its cities become more crowed. Farming methods are inefficient and there is not enough money to pipe water to the desert areas to grow more crops. Millions of Mexicans do not have jobs.

Yet, there are good signs. Starvation and disease are less common in Mexico than in other Central American countries. Mexican economics and politics are also fairly stable compared to countries farther south. There are great mineral riches for the future.

The Mexican people are still hopeful for the future, in spite of the many economic setbacks their country has experienced. They are willing to learn and work hard. Mexico has to deal with its economic problems and pay its debts to improve the country's standard of living. To do this the nation must take advantage of all its resources, including its people.

Getting ahead

For many Mexicans, getting ahead means moving, whether it is leaving a village to look for work in a large city or town, leaving a city to go where the jobs are, or leaving Mexico entirely. Mexico City is a big attraction. It is estimated that each day more than 1,000 people move there. Some Mexicans leave for cities on the Gulf Coast, looking for work in the oil industry. Others head for coastal towns with booming tourist industries. Border towns where foreign companies have opened factories to take advantage of low-cost labor are another destination.

Many other Mexicans head north to the American border, and try to enter the U.S. illegally. These people are usually looking for work with the hope of sending money home to their families. It is estimated that as many as four million Mexicans cross into the U.S. each year. Many are traveling illegally and are caught by border patrols (above right).

The quake of '85

In September 1985 a gigantic earthquake destroyed areas of Mexico City and nearby towns. Earthquakes and volcanic eruptions are regular setbacks that use up immense sums of money in disaster relief and rebuilding.

A bright future?

Dusk falls on the world's largest city, and the hopes of the people shine as brightly as the lights. Mexico City can give you anything you want – provided you can pay for it.

Citizens of the future

Millions of Mexican children from the shanty towns dream of getting a good job in a modern city, and perhaps having their own house and car. If the government's plans for industry and construction succeed, these hopes could come true.

Index

Acknowledgments

All illustrations by Ann Savage.
Photographic credits (a = above, b = below, m = middle, l = left, r = right):
Cover al Benser/Zefa, bl Formenti/Mexican Tourist Authority, ar Zefa, br Damm/Zefa; page 8 Steenmans/Zefa; page 9 Grathwohl/ Zefa; page 12 James Carmichael/NHPA; page 13 Tony Hutchings; page 14 Schorken/Zefa; page 15 a Benser/Zefa, b Benser/Zefa; page 17 Sean Sprague/Mexicolore; page 18 Tony Morrison/ South American Pictures; page 19 Tony Morrison/ South American Pictures; page 20 a David Pearson, b McAllister/Zefa; page 21 Bond/Zefa; page 22 Goebel/Zefa; page 23 Mexicolore; page 24 David Pearson; page 25 Damm/Zefa; page 29 a Benser/ Zefa, b BPCC/Aldus Archive; page 32 Sean Sprague/Mexicolore; page 33 al Sean Sprague/Mexicolore, br BPCC/Aldus Archive; page 34 Daily Telegraph Colour Library; page 35 a Tony Morrison/ South American Pictures, b Zeidl/Zefa; page 36 Sean Sprague/ Mexicolore; page 37 BPCC/Aldus Archive; page 38 Tony Hutchings; page 39 David Pearson; page 40 David Pearson; page 41 a Tony Morrison, b Grathwohl/Zefa; page 42 Dagli Orti/E.T. Archive; page 43 Schmied/Zefa; page 44 Tony Morrison/ South American Pictures; page 45 a Earl Young/Robert Harding Picture Library, b Benser/Zefa.